A Study
on
Dispensationalism

By

Arthur W. Pink

www.gideonhousebooks.com

Contents

Biography of A.W. Pink

Pink was born in Nottingham, England on April 1, 1886 and became a Christian in 1908, at the age of 22. Though born to Christian parents, prior to conversion he migrated into a Theosophical society (an occult gnostic group popular in England during that time), and quickly rose in prominence within their ranks. His conversion came from his father's patient admonitions from Scripture. It was the verse, Proverbs 14:12, 'there is a way which seemeth right unto a man, but the end thereof are the ways of death,' which particularly struck his heart and compelled him to renounce Theosophy and follow Jesus.

Desiring to grow in knowledge of the Bible, Pink emigrated to the United States to study at Moody Bible Institute. Impatient, he left there after only two months and began his first pastorate in Silverton Colorado. In 1916 he married Vera E. Russell (January 8, 1893 - July 17, 1962), who was from Kentucky. However, he left after just two months for Colorado, then California, then Britain. From 1925 to 1928 he served in Australia, including as pastor of two congregations from 1926 to 1928, when he returned to England, and to the United States the following year. He eventually pastored churches in Colorado, California, Kentucky, and South Carolina.

In January 1922 he started a monthly magazine entitled *Studies in the Scriptures* which circulated among English-speaking Christians worldwide, though only to a relatively small circulation list of around 1,000.

In 1934 Pink returned to England, and within a few years turned his Christian service to writing books and pamphlets. Pink died in Stornoway, Scotland on July 15, 1952. The cause of death was anemia.

After Pink's death, his works were republished by a number of publishing houses, among them, Banner of Truth Trust, Baker Book House, Christian Focus Publications, Moody Press, Truth for Today, and reached a much wider audience as a result. Biographer Iain Murray observes of Pink, "the widespread circulation of his writings after his death made him one of the most influential evangelical authors in the second half of the twentieth century." His writing sparked a revival of expository preaching and focused readers' hearts on biblical living. Yet, even today, Pink is left out of most biographical dictionaries and overlooked in many religious histories. (Source: Wikipedia)

Chapter 1

Having written so much upon both the inspiration and the interpretation of Holy Writ, it is necessary, in order to give completeness unto the same, to supply one or two articles upon the application thereof. First, because this is very closely related to exegesis itself: if a wrong application or use be made of a verse, then our explanation of it is certain to be erroneous. For example, Romanism insists that "Feed my sheep" (John 21:15-17) was Christ's bestowal upon Peter of a special privilege and peculiar honour, being one of the passages to which that evil system appeals in support of her contention for *the primacy* of that Apostle. Yet there is nothing whatever in Peter's own writings which indicates that he regarded those injunctions of his Master as constituting him "Universal Bishop." Instead, in his first Epistle there is plainly that to the contrary, for there we find him exhorting the elders or bishops, "Feed the flock of God which is among you, taking the oversight thereof, not by constraint, but willingly; not for filthy lucre, but of a ready mind; neither as being lords over God's heritage, but being ensamples to the flock" (5:2,3).

Thus it is quite clear from the above passage that Christ's precepts in John 21:15-17, apply or pertain unto *all pastors*. On the other hand, our Lord's words to Peter and Andrew, "Follow Me, and I will make you fishers of men" (Matt. 4:19) *do not* apply to the rank and file of His disciples, but only unto those whom He calls into and qualifies for the ministry. That is evident from the fact that in none of the Epistles, where both the privileges and the duties of the saints are specifically defined, is there any such precept or promise. Thus, on the one hand, we must ever beware of unwarrantable restricting the scope of a verse; and, on the other hand, be constantly on our guard against making general what is manifestly particular. It is only by carefully taking heed to the general Analogy of Faith that we shall be preserved from either mistake. Scripture ever interprets Scripture, but much familiarity with the contents, and a diligent and prayerful comparing of one part with another, is necessary before anyone is justified in dogmatically deciding the precise meaning or application of any passage.

But there is further reason, and a pressing one today, why we should write upon our present subject, and that is to expose the modern and pernicious error of Dispensationalism. This is a device of the Enemy, designed to rob the children of no small part of that bread which their heavenly Father has provided for their souls; a device wherein the wily serpent appears as an angel of light, feigning to "make the Bible a new book" by simplifying much in it which perplexes the spiritually unlearned. It is sad to see how widely successful the devil has been by means of this subtle innovation. It is likely that some of our own readers, when perusing the articles upon the interpretation of the Scriptures, felt more than once that we were taking an undue liberty with Holy Writ, that we made use of certain passages in a way altogether unjustifiable, that we appropriated to the saints of this Christian era what does not belong to them but is rather addressed unto those who lived in an entirely different dispensation of the past, or one which is yet future.

This modern method of mishandling the Scriptures—for modern it certainly is, being quite unknown to Christendom till little more than a century ago, and only within recent years being adopted by those who are outside the narrow circle where it originated—is based upon 2 Timothy 2:15, "Study to show thyself approved unto God, a workman that needeth not to be ashamed, rightly dividing the word of truth." Very little or nothing at all is said upon the first two clauses of that verse, but on the third one, which is explained as "correctly partitioning the Scriptures unto the different peoples to whom they belong." These mutilators of the Word tell us that all of the Old Testament from Genesis 12 onwards belongs entirely to Israel after the flesh, and that none of its precepts (as such) are binding upon those who are members of the Church which is the Body of Christ, nor may any of the promises found therein be legitimately appropriated

8

by them. And this, be it duly noted, *without* a single word to that effect by either the Lord or any of His Apostles, *and despite* the use which the Holy Spirit makes of the earliest Scriptures in every part of the New Testament. So far from the Holy Spirit teaching Christians practically to look upon the Old Testament much as they would upon an obsolete almanac, He declares, "For whatsoever things were written aforetime were written for *our learning*, that we through patience and comfort of the (Old Testament) Scriptures might have hope" (Rom. 15:4).

Not satisfied with their determined efforts to deprive us of the Old Testament, these would-be super-expositors dogmatically assert that the four Gospels are Jewish, and that the Epistles of James and Peter, John and Jude are designed for a "godly Jewish remnant" in a future "tribulation period," that nothing but the Pauline Epistles contain "Church truth," and thousands of gullible souls have accepted their *ipse digit*—those who decline so doing are regarded as untaught and superficial. Yet God Himself has not uttered a single word to that effect. Certainly there is nothing whatever in 2 Timothy 2:15, to justify such a revolutionizing method of interpreting the Word: that verse has no more to do with the sectioning of Scripture between different "dispensations" than it has with distinguishing between stars of varying magnitude. If that verse be carefully compared with Matthew 7:6, John 16:12 and 1 Corinthians 3:2, its meaning is clear. The occupant of the pulpit is to give diligence in becoming equipped to give the different classes of his hearer "their *portion of meat* in due season" (Luke 12:42). To rightly divide the Word of Truth is for him to minister it suitably unto the several cases and circumstances of his congregation: to sinners and saints, the indifferent and the inquiring, the babes and fathers, the tempted and afflicted, the backslidden and fallen.

While there be great variety in the teaching of the Word, there is an unmistakable unity underlying the whole. Though He employed many mouthpieces, the Holy Scriptures have but one Author; and while He "at sundry times and in divers manners spake in time past unto the fathers by the prophets" and "hath in these last days spoken unto us by His Son" (Heb. 1:1,2), yet He who spoke by them was and is One "with whom is no variableness, neither shadow of turning" (Jam. 1:17), who throughout all ages declares: "I am the Lord, I change not" (Mal. 3:6). Throughout there is

9

perfect agreement between every part of the Word: it sets forth *one system of doctrine* (we never read of "the doctrines of God," but always "the doctrine": see Deut 32:2; Prov 4:2; Matt 7:28; John 7:17; Rom. 16:17, and contrast Mark 7:7; Col. 2:22; 1 Tim. 4:1; Heb. 13:9) because it is one single and organic whole. That Word presents uniformly *one* way of salvation, *one* rule of faith. From Genesis to Revelation there is one immutable Moral Law, one glorious Gospel for perishing sinners. The Old Testament believers were saved with the same salvation, were indebted to the same Redeemer, were renewed by the same Spirit, and were partakers of the same heavenly inheritance as are New Testament believers.

It is quite true that the Epistle to the Hebrews makes mention of a better hope (7:19), a better testament or covenant (7:22), better promises (8:6), better sacrifices (9:23), some better thing for us (11:40), and yet it is important to recognize that the contrast is between *the shadows and the substance*. Romans 12:6, speaks of "the proportion [or "analogy"] of faith." There is a due proportion, a perfect balance, between the different parts of God's revealed Truth which must needs be known and observed by all who would preach and write according to the mind of the Spirit. In arguing from this analogy, it is essential to recognize that what is made known in the Old Testament was *typical* of what is set forth in the New, and therefore the terms used in the former are strictly applicable unto the latter. Much needless wrangling has occurred over whether or not the nation of Israel were a regenerate people. That is quite beside the real point: outwardly they were regarded and addressed as the people of God, and, as the Spirit through Paul affirmed, "who are Israelites: to whom pertaineth the adoption, and the glory, and the covenants, and the giving of the law, and the service of God, and the promises: whose are the fathers, and of whom as concerning the flesh Christ came" (Rom. 9:4,5).

Regeneration or non-regeneration affected the salvation of *individuals* among them, but it did not affect the covenant relationship of the people *as a whole*. Again and again God addressed Israel as "backsliders," but never once did He so designate any heathen nation. It was not to the Egyptians or Canaanites that Jehovah said, "Return, ye backsliding *children,* and I will heal your backslidings," or "Turn, 0 backsliding children… for I am *married unto you*" (Jer. 3:22, 14). Now it is this analogy or similarity between

10

the two covenants and the peoples under them which is the basis for the transfer of Old Testament terms to the New. Thus the word "circumcision" is used in the latter not with identity of meaning, but according to analogy, for circumcision is now "of the heart, in the spirit" (Rom. 2:29), and not of the flesh. In like manner, when John closes his first Epistle with "Little children, keep yourselves from idols," he borrows an Old Testament term and uses it in a New Testament sense, for by "idols" he refers not to material statues made of wood and stone (as the prophets did when employing the same word), but to inward objects of carnal and sensual worship. So too are we to see the antitypical and spiritual "Israel" in Galatians 6:16, and the celestial and eternal "Mount Zion" in Hebrews 12:22.

The Bible consists of many parts, exquisitely correlated and vitally interdependent upon each other. God so controlled all the agents which He employed in the writing of it, and so coordinated their efforts, as to produce a single living Book. Within that organic unity there is indeed much variety, but no contrariety. Man's body is but one, though it be made up of many members, diverse in size, character, and operation. The rainbow is but one, nevertheless it reflects distinctly the seven prismatic rays, yet they are harmoniously blended together. So it is with the Bible: its unity appears in the perfect consistency throughout of its teachings. The oneness yet triunity of God, the deity and humanity of Christ united in one Person, the everlasting covenant which secures the salvation of all the election of grace, the highway of holiness and the only path which leads to heaven, are plainly revealed in Old and New Testament alike. The teaching of the prophets concerning the glorious character of God, the changeless requirements of His righteousness, the total depravity of human nature, and the way appointed for restoration therefrom, are identical with the Apostles' teaching.

If the question be raised, Since the sacred Scriptures be a strict unit, then why has God Himself divided them into two Testaments? perhaps it will simplify the matter if we ask why God has appointed two principal bodies to illuminate the earth—the sun and the moon. Why, too, is the human frame duplex, having two legs and arms, two lungs and kidneys, etc.? Is not the answer the same in each case: to augment and supplement each other? But, more directly, at least four reasons may be suggested. First, to set forth more distinctly the two covenants which are the basis of God's dealings with all mankind: the covenant of works and the covenant of grace—shadowed forth by the "old" from Sinai and the "new" or Christian one. Second, to show more plainly the two separate companies which are united in that one Body which constitutes the Church of which Christ is the Head, namely redeemed Jews and redeemed Gentiles. Third, to demonstrate more clearly the wondrous providence of God: using the Jews for so many centuries to be the custodians of the Old Testament, which condemns them for their rejection of Christ; and in employing the papists throughout the dark ages to preserve the New Testament, which denounces their idolatrous practices. Fourth, that one might confirm the other: type by antitype, prophecy by fulfillment.

"The mutual relations of the two Testaments. These two main divisions resemble the dual structure of the human body, where the two eyes and ears, hands and feet, correspond to and complement one another. Not only is there a general, but a special, mutual fitness. They need therefore to be studied together, side by side, to be compared even in lesser details, for in nothing are they independent of each other; and the closer the inspection the minuter appears the adaptation, and the more intimate the association… .The two Testaments are like the two cherubim of the mercy seat, facing in opposite directions, yet facing each other and overshadowing with glory one mercy seat; or again, they are like the human body bound together by joints and bands and ligaments, with one brain and heart, one pair of lungs, one system of respiration, circulation, digestion, sensor and motor nerves, where division is destruction" (A. T. Pierson, from *Knowing the Scriptures*).

Chapter 2

Some Dispensationalists do not go quite so far as others in arbitrarily erecting notice-boards over large sections of Scripture, warning Christians not to tread on ground which belongs to others, yet there is general agreement among them that the Gospel of Matthew—though it stands at the beginning of the New Testament and not at the close of the Old!—pertains not to those who are members of the mystical body of Christ, but is "entirely Jewish," that the sermon on the mount is "legalistic" and not evangelistic, and that its searching and flesh-withering precepts are not binding upon Christians. Some go so far as to insist that the great commission with which it closes is not designed for us today, but is meant for "a godly Jewish remnant" after the present era is ended. In support of this wild and wicked theory, appeal is made to and great stress laid upon the fact that Christ is represented, most prominently, as "the son of David" or King of the Jews; but they ignore another conspicuous fact, namely that in its opening verse the Lord Jesus is set forth as "the son of Abraham," and *he* was a *Gentile!* What is still more against this untenable hypothesis—and as though the Holy Spirit designedly anticipated and refuted it—is the fact that Matthew's is the only one of the four Gospels where the Church is actually mentioned twice (16:18; 18:17)!—though in John's Gospel its members are portrayed as branches of the Vine, members of Christ's flock, which are designations of saints which have no dispensational limitations.

Equally remarkable is the fact that the very same Epistle which contains the verse (2 Tim. 2:15) on which this modern system is based emphatically declares: "*All Scripture* is given by inspiration of God, and is profitable for doctrine, for reproof, for correction, for instruction in righteousness; that the man of God may be perfect, thoroughly furnished unto all good works" (3:16,17). So far from large sections of Scripture being designed for other companies, and excluded from our immediate use, ALL Scripture is meant for and is needed by us. First, all of it is "profitable for doctrine," which could not be the case if it were true (as Dispensationalists dogmatically insist) that God has entirely different methods of dealing with men in past and future ages from the present one. Second, all Scripture is given us "for instruction in righteousness" or right doing, but we are at a complete loss to know how to regulate our conduct if the precepts in one part of the Bible are now outdated (as the teachers of error assert) and injunctions of a contrary character have displaced them; and if certain statutes are meant for others who will occupy this scene after the Church has been removed from it. Third, all Scripture is given that a man of God might be "perfect, thoroughly furnished unto all good works"—every part of the Word is required in order to supply him with all needed instructions and to produce a full-orbed life of godliness.

When the Dispensationalist is hard pressed with those objections, he endeavors to wriggle out of his dilemma by declaring that though all Scripture be *for* us much of it is not addressed *to* us. But really, that is a distinction without a difference. In his exposition of Hebrews 3:7-11, Owen rightly pointed out that when making quotation from the Old Testament the Apostle prefaced it with "the Holy Spirit saith" (not "said"), and remarked, "Whatever was given by inspiration from the Holy Spirit and is recorded in the Scriptures for the use of the Church, He contrived to speak it to us unto this day. As He liveth for ever so He continues to speak for ever; that is, whilst His voice or word shall be of use for the Church—*He speaks now unto us* ... .Many men have invented several ways to lessen the authority of the Scriptures, and few are willing to acknowledge an *immediate* speaking of God unto them therein." To the same effect wrote that sound commentator Thomas Scott, "Because of the immense advantages of perseverance, and the tremendous consequences of apostasy, we should consider the words of the Holy Spirit as addressed to us."

Not only is the assertion that though all Scripture be *for us* all is *not to us* meaningless, but it is also *impertinent* and impudent, for there is nothing whatever in the Word of Truth to support and substantiate it.

14

Nowhere has the Spirit given the slightest warning that such a passage is "not to the Christian," and still less that whole books belong to someone else. Moreover, such a principle is manifestly *dishonest*. What right have I to make *any use* of that which is the property of another? What would my neighbor think were I to take letters which were addressed *to* him and argue that they were meant *for* me? Furthermore, such a theory, when put to the test, is found to be *unworkable*. For example, to whom is the book of Proverbs addressed, or for that matter, the first Epistle of John? Personally, this writer, after having wasted much time in perusing scores of books which pretended to rightly divide the Word, still regards the whole of Scripture as God's gracious revelation to him and for him, as though there were not another person on earth, conscious that he cannot afford to dispense with any portion of it; and he is heartily sorry for those who lack such a faith. Pertinent in this connection is that warning, "But fear, lest by any means, as the serpent beguiled Eve … so your minds should be corrupted *from the simplicity* that is in Christ" (2 Cor. 11:3).

But are there not many passages in the Old Testament which have no direct bearing upon the Church today? Certainly not. In view of 1 Corinthians 10:11—"Now all these things happened unto them for ensamples [margin, "types"]: and they are written for our admonition"— Owen pithily remarked: "Old Testament examples are New Testament instructions." By their histories we are taught what to avoid and what to emulate. That is the principal reason why they are *recorded*: that which hindered or encouraged the Old Testament saints was chronicled for our benefit. But, more specifically, are not Christians unwarranted in applying to themselves many promises given to Israel according to the flesh during the Mosaic economy, and expecting a fulfillment of the same unto themselves? No indeed, for if *that* were the case, then it would not be true that "whatsoever things were written aforetime were written for our learning, that we through patience and comfort of the scriptures might have hope" (Rom. 15:4). What comfort can I derive from those sections of God's Word which these people say "do not belong to me"? What "hope" (i.e. a well-grounded assurance of some future good) could possibly be inspired today in Christians by what pertains to none but Jews? Christ came here, my reader, not to cancel, but "to *confirm* the promises made

15

unto the fathers: and that the *Gentiles* might glorify God for His mercy" (Rom. 15:8,9)!

It must also be borne in mind that, in keeping with the character of the covenant under which they were made, many of the precepts and the promises given unto the patriarchs and their descendants possessed a *spiritual and typical* significance and value, as well as a carnal and literal one. As an example of the former, take Deuteronomy 25:4, "Thou shalt not muzzle the ox when he treadeth out the corn," and then mark the application made of those words in 1 Corinthians 9:9,10: "Doth God take care for oxen? Or saith He it altogether for our *sakes*? For our sakes, no doubt, this is written: that he that ploweth should plow in hope." The word "altogether" is probably a little too strong here, for pantos is rendered "no doubt" in Acts 28:4, and "surely" in Luke 4:23, and in the text signifies "assuredly" (Amer. RV) or "*mainly* for our sakes." Deuteronomy 25:4 was designed to enforce the principle that labour should have its reward, so that men might work cheerfully. The precept enjoined equity and kindness: if so to beasts, much more so to men, and especially the ministers of the Gospel. It is a striking illustration of the freedom with which the Spirit of grace applies the Old Testament Scriptures, as a constituent part of the Word of Christ, unto Christians and their concerns.

What is true of the Old Testament precepts (generally speaking, for there are, of course, exceptions to every rule) holds equally good to the Old Testament promises—believers today are fully warranted in mixing faith therewith and expecting to receive the substance of them. First, because those promises were made to saints as such, and what God gives to one He gives to all (2 Pet. 1:4)—Christ purchased the self-same blessings for every one of His redeemed. Second, because most of the Old Testament promises were typical in their nature: earthly blessings adumbrated heavenly ones. That is no arbitrary assertion of ours, for anyone who has been taught of God knows that almost everything during the old economies had a figurative meaning, shadowing forth the better things to come. Many proofs of this will be given by us a little later. Third, a *literal* fulfillment to us of those promises must not be excluded, for since we be still on earth and in the body our temporal needs are the same as theirs, and if we meet the conditions attached to those promises (either expressed or implied), then we may count upon the fulfillment of them: according unto our faith and obedience so will it be unto us.

But surely we must draw a definite and broad line between the Law and the Gospel. It is at this point that the Dispensationalist considers his position to be the strongest and most unassailable; yet nowhere else does he more display his ignorance, for he neither recognizes the grace of God abounding during the Mosaic era, nor can he see that Law has any rightful place in this Christian age. Law and grace are to him antagonistic elements, and (to quote one of his favorite slogans) "will no more mix than will oil and water." Not a few of those who are now regarded as the champions of orthodoxy tell their hearers that the principles of law and grace are such contrary elements that where the one be in exercise the other must necessarily be excluded. But this is a very serious error. How could the Law *of God* and the Gospel of the grace *of God* conflict? The one exhibits Him as "light," the other manifest Him as "love" (1 John 1:5; 4:8), and both are necessary in order fully to reveal His perfections: if either one be omitted only a one-sided concept of His character will be formed. The one makes known His righteousness, the other displays His mercy, and His wisdom has shown the perfect consistency there is between them.

Instead of law and grace being contradictory, they are complementary. Both of them appeared in Eden before the Fall. What was it but grace which made a grant unto our first parents: "Of every tree of the garden thou mayest freely eat"? And it was law which said, "But of the tree of knowledge of good and evil, thou shalt not eat of it." Both of them are seen at the time of the great deluge, for we are told that "Noah found grace in the eyes of the Lord" (Gen. 6:8), as His subsequent dealings with him clearly demonstrated; while His righteousness brought in a flood upon the world of the ungodly. Both of them operated side by side at Sinai, for while the majesty and righteousness of Jehovah were expressed in the Decalogue, His mercy and grace were plainly evinced in the provisions He made in the whole Levitical system (with its priesthood and sacrifices) for the putting away of their sins. Both shone forth in their meridian glory at Calvary, for whereas on the one hand the abounding grace of God appeared in giving His own dear Son to be the Saviour of sinners, His justice called for the curse of the Law to be inflicted upon Him while bearing their guilt.

In all of God's works and ways we may discern a meeting together of *seemingly* conflicting elements—the centrifugal and the centripetal forces which are ever at work in the material realm illustrate this principle. So it is in connection with the operations of Divine providence: there is a constant interpenetrating of the natural and supernatural. So too in the giving of the sacred Scriptures: they are the product both of God's and man's agency: they are a Divine revelation, yet couched in human language, and communicated through human media; they are inerrantly true, yet written by fallible men. They are Divinely inspired in every jot and tittle, yet the superintending control of the Spirit over the penmen did not exclude nor interfere with the natural exercise of their faculties. Thus it is also in all of God's dealings with mankind: though He exercises His high sovereignty, yet He treats with them as responsible creatures, putting forth His invincible power upon and within them, but in no wise destroying their moral agency. These may present deep and insoluble mysteries to the finite mind, nevertheless they are actual facts.

In what has just been pointed out—to which other examples might be added (the person of Christ, for instance, with His two distinct yet conjoined natures, so that though He was omniscient yet He "grew in wisdom"; was omnipotent, yet wearied and slept; was eternal, yet died)— why should so many stumble at the phenomenon of Divine law and Divine grace being in exercise side by side, operating at the same season? Do law and grace present any greater contrast than the fathomless love of God unto His children, and His everlasting wrath upon His enemies? No indeed, not so great. Grace must not be regarded as an attribute of God which eclipses all His other perfections. As Romans 5:21 so plainly tells us, "That as sin hath reigned unto death, even so might grace reign *through righteousness*," and not at the expense of or to the exclusion of it. Divine grace and Divine righteousness, Divine love and Divine holiness, are as inseparable as light and heat from the sun. In bestowing grace, God never rescinds His claims upon us, but rather enables us to meet them. Was the prodigal son, after his penitential return and forgiveness, less obliged to conform to the laws of his Father's house than before he left it? No indeed, but more so.

That there is no conflict between the Law and the Gospel of the grace of God is plain enough in Romans 3:31: "Do we then make void the law through faith? God forbid: yea, we establish the law." Here the Apostle anticipates an objection which was likely to be brought against what he said in verses 26-30. Does not the teaching that justification is entirely by grace through faith evince that God has relaxed His claims, changed the standard of His requirements, set aside the demands of His government? Very far from it. The Divine plan of redemption is in no way an annulling of the Law, but rather the honoring and enforcing of it. No greater respect could have been shown to the Law than in God's determining to save His people from its course by sending His co-equal Son to fulfill all its requirements and Himself endure its penalty. Oh, marvel of marvels; the great Legislator humbled Himself unto entire obedience to the precepts of the Decalogue. The very One who gave the Law became incarnate, bled and died, under its condemning sentence, rather than that a tittle thereof should fail. Magnified thus was the Law indeed, and for ever "made honorable."

God's method of salvation by grace has "established the law" in a threefold way. First, by Christ, the Surety of God's elect, being "made under the law" (Gal. 4:4), fulfilling its precepts (Matt. 5:17), suffering its penalty in the stead of His people, and thereby He has "brought everlasting righteousness" (Dan. 9:24). Second, by the Holy Spirit, for at regeneration He writes the Law on their hearts (Heb. 8:10), drawing out their affections unto it, so that they "delight in the law of God after the inward man" (Rom. 7:22). Third, as the fruit of his new nature, the Christian voluntarily and gladly takes the Law for his rule of life, so that he declares, "with the mind I myself *serve* the law" (Rom. 7:25). Thus is the Law "established" not only in the high court of heaven, but in the souls of the redeemed. So far from law and grace being enemies, they are mutual handmaids: the former reveals the sinner's need, the latter supplies it; the one makes known God's requirements, the other enables us to meet them. Faith is not opposed to good works, but performs them in obedience to God out of love and gratitude.

Chapter 3

Before turning to the positive side of our present subject, it was necessary for us to expose and denounce that teaching which insists that much in the Bible has no immediate application unto us today. Such teaching is a reckless and irreverent handling of the Word, which has produced the most evil consequences in the hearts and lives of many—not the least of which is the promotion of a pharisaical spirit of self-superiority. Consciously or unconsciously, Dispensationalists are, in reality, repeating the sin of Jehoiakim, who mutilated God's Word with his penknife (Jer 36:23). Instead of "opening the Scriptures," they are bent in closing the major part of them from God's people today. They are just as much engaged in doing the devil's work as are the Higher Critics, who, with their dissecting knives, are *wrongly* "dividing the word of truth." They are seeking to force a stone down the throats of those who are asking for bread. These are indeed severe and solemn indictments, but not more so than the case calls for. We are well aware that they will be unacceptable unto some of our own readers; but medicine, though sometimes necessary, is rarely palatable.

Instead of being engaged in the unholy work of pitting one part of the Scriptures against another, these men would be far better employed in showing the perfect *unity* of the Bible and the blessed harmony which there is between all of its teachings. But instead of demonstrating the concord of the two Testaments, they are more concerned in their efforts to show the discord which they say there is between that which pertained unto "the Dispensation of Law" and that which obtains under "the Dispensation of Grace," and in order to accomplish their evil design all sound principles of exegesis are cast to the wind. As a sample of what we have reference to, they cite "Eye for eye, tooth for tooth, hand for hand, foot for foot" (Ex. 21:24) and then quote against it, "But I say unto you, That ye resist not evil: but whosoever shall smite thee on thy right cheek, turn to him the other also" (Matt. 5:39), and then it is exultantly asserted that those two passages can only be "reconciled" by allocating them to different peoples in different ages; and with such superficial handling of Holy Writ thousands of gullible souls are deceived, and thousands more allow themselves to be bewildered.

If those who possess a *Scofield Bible* turn to Exodus 21:24, they will see that in the margin opposite to it the editor refers his readers to Leviticus 24:20; Deuteronomy 19:21, and cf. Matthew 5:28-44; 1 Peter 2:19-21; upon which this brief comment is made: "The provision in Exodus is *law* and righteous; the New Testament passages, grace and merciful." How far Mr. Scofield was consistent with himself may be seen by a reference to what he states on page 989, at the beginning of the New Testament under the Four Gospels, where he expressly affirms "The sermon on the mount is law, *not grace*" [italics ours]: verily "the legs of the lame are not equal." In his marginal note to Exodus 21:24, Mr. Scofield cites Matthew 5:38-44, as "grace," whereas in his introduction to the Four Gospels he declares that Matthew 5-7 "is law, and not grace." Which of those assertions did he wish his readers to believe?

Still the question may be asked, How are *you* going to reconcile Exodus 21:24, with Matthew 5:38-44? Our answer is, There is nothing between them *to* "reconcile," for there is nothing in them which clashes. The former passage is one of the statutes appointed for *public magistrates* to enforce, whereas the latter one lays down rules *for private individuals* to live by! Why do not these self-styled "rightly dividers" properly allocate the Scriptures, distinguishing between the different classes to which they are addressed? That Exodus 21:24 does contain statutes for public magistrates to enforce is clearly established by comparing Scripture with Scripture. In Deuteronomy 19:21, the same injunction is again recorded, and if the reader turns back to verse 18 he will there read, "And *the judges* shall make diligent inquisition," etc. It would be real mercy unto the community if our judges today would set aside their sickly sentimentality and deal with conscienceless and brutal criminals in a manner which befits their deeds of violence—instead of making a mockery of justice.

Ere leaving what has been before us in the last three paragraphs, let it be pointed out that when our blessed Lord added to Matthew 5:38, "But I say unto you, Love your enemies, bless them that curse you, do good to them that hate you" (verse 44) He was not advancing a more benign precept than had ever been enunciated previously. No, the same gracious principle of conduct had been enforced in the Old Testament. In Exodus 23:4, 5, Jehovah gave commandment through Moses, "If thou meet thine *enemy's* ox or his ass going astray, thou shalt surely bring it back to him again. If thou see the ass of him that hateth thee lying under his burden, and wouldest forbear to help him, thou shalt surely help with him." Again in Proverbs 25:21, we read, "If thine enemy be hungry, give him bread to eat; and if he be thirsty, give him water to drink."

The same God who bids us, "Recompense to no man evil for evil. Provide things honest in the sight of all men. If it be possible, as much as lieth in you, live peaceably with all men. Dearly beloved, avenge not yourselves, but rather give place unto wrath" (Rom. 12:17-19), also commanded His people in the *Old* Testament, "Thou shalt *not avenge*, nor bear any grudge against the children of thy people, but thou shalt love thy neighbour as thyself: I am the Lord" (Lev. 19:18); and therefore was David grateful to Abigail for dissuading him from taking vengeance on Nabal: "Blessed be thou, which hast kept me this day from coming to shed blood, and from avenging myself with mine own hand" (1 Sam. 25:33). So far was the Old Testament from allowing any spirit of bitterness, malice or revenge that it expressly declared, "Say not thou, I will recompense evil; but wait on the Lord, and He shall save thee" (Prov. 20:22). And again, "*Rejoice not* when thine enemy falleth, and let not thine heart be glad when he stumbleth" (Prov. 24:17). And again, "Say not, I will do so to him as he hath done to me: I will render to the man according to his work" (Prov. 24:29).

One more sample of the excuseless ignorance betrayed by these Dispensationalists—we quote from E.W. Bullinger's *How to Enjoy the Bible*. On pages 108 and 110 he said under "Law and Grace": "For those who lived under the Law it could rightly and truly be said, 'It shall be our righteousness, if we observe to do all these commandments before the Lord our God, as He hath commanded us' (Deut 6:25). But to those who live in this present Dispensation of Grace it is as truly declared, 'By the deeds of the law there shall no flesh be justified in His sight' (Rom. 3:20). But this is the very opposite of Deuteronomy 6:25. What, then, are we to say, or to do? Which of these two statements is true and which is false? The answer is that neither is false. But both are true if we would rightly divide the Word of Truth as to its dispensational truth and teaching... .Two words distinguish the two dispensations: 'Do' distinguished the former; 'Done' the latter. Then salvation depended upon what man was *to do*, now it depends upon what Christ has done." It is by such statements as these that "unstable souls" are beguiled.

Is it not amazing that one so renowned for his erudition and knowledge of the Scriptures should make such manifestly absurd statements as the above? In pitting Deuteronomy 6:25 against Romans 3:20, he might as well have argued that fire is "the very opposite" of water. They are indeed contrary elements, yet each has its own use in its proper place: the one to cook by, the other for refreshment. Think of one who set up himself as a teacher of preachers affirming that under the Mosaic economy "salvation depended on what man was to do." Why, in that case, for fifteen hundred years not a single Israelite had been saved. Had salvation then been obtainable by human efforts, there had been no need for God to send His Son here! Salvation has never been procurable by human merits, on the ground of human performance. Abel obtained witness that he was righteous, because he offered to God a slain lamb (Gen. 4:4; Heb. 11:4). Abraham was justified by faith, and not by works (Romans 4). Under the Mosaic economy it was expressly announced that "it is the blood that maketh an atonement for the soul" (Lev. 17:11). David realized, "If Thou, Lord, shouldest mark iniquities, 0 Lord, who shall stand?" (Ps. 130:3); and therefore did he confess, "I will make mention of Thy righteousness, even of *Thine only*" (Ps. 71:16).

By all means let the Word of Truth be "rightly divided"; not by parceling it off to different "dispensations," but by distinguishing between what is doctrinal and what is *practical*, between that which pertains to the unsaved and that which is predicated of the saved. Deuteronomy 6:25 is addressed not to alien sinners, but to those who are in covenant relationship with the Lord; whereas Romans 3:20 is a statement which applies to every member of the human race. The one has to do with practical "righteousness" in the daily walk, which is acceptable to God; the other is a doctrinal declaration which asserts the impossibility of acceptance with God on the ground of creature doings. The former relates to our conduct in this life in connection with the Divine government; the latter concerns our eternal standing before the Divine throne. Both passages are equally applicable to Jews and Gentiles in all ages. "Our righteousness" in Deuteronomy 6:25 is a practical righteousness in the sight of God. It is the same aspect of righteousness as in "except your righteousness exceed the righteousness of the scribes and Pharisees" of Matthew 5:20, the "righteous man" of James 5:16, and the "doeth righteousness" of 1 John 2:29.

The Old Testament saints were the subjects of the same everlasting covenant, had the same blessed Gospel, were begotten unto the same celestial heritage as the New Testament saints. From Abel onwards, God has dealt with sinners in sovereign grace, and according to the merits of Christ's redemptive work—which was retroactive in its value and efficacy (Romans 3:25; 1 Peter 1:19,20). "Noah found grace in the eyes of the Lord" (Gen. 6:8). That they were partakers of the same covenant blessings as we are is clear from a comparison of 2 Samuel 23:5, and Hebrews 13:20. The same Gospel was preached unto Abraham (Gal. 3:8), yea, unto the nation of Israel after they had received the Law (Heb 4:2), and therefore Abraham rejoiced to see Christ's day and was glad (John 8:56). Dying Jacob declared, "I have waited for Thy salvation, 0 Lord" (Gen. 49:18). As Hebrews 11:16 states, the patriarchs *desired* "a better country [than the land of Canaan, in which they dwelt], that is, an heavenly." Moses "refused to be called the son of Pharaoh's daughter… esteeming the reproach *of Christ* greater riches than the treasures of Egypt" (Heb. 11:24-26). Job exclaimed, "I know that my Redeemer liveth… in my flesh shall I see God" (19:25,26).

When Jehovah proclaimed His name unto Moses, He revealed Himself as "the Lord, the Lord God, *merciful and gracious*" (Exo 34:5-7). When Aaron pronounced the benediction on the congregation, he was bidden to say, "The Lord bless thee, and keep thee: the Lord make His face shine upon thee, and be gracious unto thee: the Lord lift up His countenance upon thee, and give thee peace" (Num. 6:24-26). No greater and grander blessings can be invoked today. Such a passage as that cannot possibly be harmonized with the constricted concept which is entertained and is being propagated by the Dispensationalists of the Mosaic economy. God dealt *in grace* with Israel all through their long and checkered history. Read through the book of Judges and observe how often He raised up deliverers for them. Pass on to Kings and Chronicles and note His longsuffering benignity in sending them prophet after prophet. Where in the New Testament is there a word which, for pure grace, exceeds "though your sins be as scarlet, they shall be as white as snow" (Isa 1:18)? In the days of Jehoahaz "the Lord was gracious unto them" (2 Kings 13:22-23). They were invited to say unto the Lord, "Take away all iniquity, and receive us graciously" (Hosea 14:2). Malachi bade Israel "beseech God that He will be gracious unto us" (1:9).

The conception which the pious remnant of Israel had of the Divine character during the Mosaic economy was radically different from the stern and forbidding presentation made thereof by Dispensationalists. Hear the Psalmist as he declared, "Gracious is the Lord, and righteous; yea, our God is merciful" (116:5). Hear him again, as he bursts forth into adoring praise, "Bless the Lord, 0 my soul, and forget not all His benefits: who forgiveth all thine iniquities, who healeth all thy diseases... He hath not dealt with us after our sins, nor rewarded us according to our iniquities" (103:2,3,10). Can Christians say more than that? No wonder David exclaimed, "Whom have I in heaven but Thee? and there is none upon earth that I desire besides Thee. My flesh and my heart faileth: but God is the strength of my heart, and my portion for ever" (73:25,26). If the question be asked, What, then, is *the great distinction* between the Mosaic and Christian eras? the answer is, God's grace was then confirmed to *one* nation, but now it flows out to *all* nations.

What is true in the general holds in the particular. Not only were God's dealings with His people during Old Testament times substantially the same as those with His people now, but *in detail* too. There is no discord, but perfect accord and concord between them. Note carefully the following parallelisms. "His inheritance in the saints" (Eph. 1:18): "The Lord's portion is His people, Jacob is the lot of His inheritance" (Deut. 32:9). "Beloved of the Lord, because God hath from the beginning chosen you to salvation" (2 Thess. 2:13): "I have loved thee with an everlasting love" (Jer. 3 1:3). "In whom we have redemption" (Eph. 1:7): "With Him is plenteous redemption" (Ps. 130:7). "That we might be made the righteousness of God *in Him*" (2 Cor. 5:2 1): "In the Lord have I righteousness and strength" (Isa. 45:24). "Who hath blessed us with all spiritual blessings… in Christ" (Eph. 1:3): "Men shall be blessed in Him" (Ps. 72:17). "The blood of Jesus Christ His Son cleanseth us from all sin" (1 John 1:7): "Thou art all fair, My love, there is *no spot* in thee" (Song 4:7).

"Strengthened with might by His Spirit in the inner man" (Eph. 3:16): "In the day when I cried Thou answeredst me, and strengthenedst me with strength in my soul" (Ps. 138:3). "The Spirit of truth … will guide you into all truth" (John 16:13): "Thou gavest also Thy good Spirit to instruct them" (Neh. 9:20). "I know that in me (that is, in my flesh), dwelleth no good thing" (Rom. 7:18): "All our righteousness are as filthy rags" (Isa. 64:6). "I beseech you as strangers and pilgrims" (1 Pet. 2:11): "Ye are strangers and sojourners" (Lev. 25:23). "We walk by faith" (2 Cor. 5:7): "The just shall live by his faith" (Hab. 2:4). "Strong in the Lord" (Eph. 6:10): "I will strengthen them in the Lord" (Zech. 10:12). "Neither shall any pluck them out of My hand" (John 10:28): "All His saints are in Thy hand" (Deut. 33:3). "He that abideth in Me, and I in him, the same bringeth forth much fruit" (John 15:5): "From Me is thy fruit found" (Hosea 14:8). "He which hath begun a good work in you will finish it" (Phil. 1:6, margin): "The Lord will perfect that which concerneth me" (Psa 138:8). Innumerable other such harmonies might be added.

Chapter 4

As it is particularly the Old Testament promises of which Dispensationalists would deprive the Christian, a more definite and detailed refutation of this error is now required—coming, as it obviously does, within the compass of our present subject. We will here transcribe what we wrote thereon almost twenty years ago.

Since the Fall alienated the creature from the Creator, there could be no intercourse between God and men but by some promise on His part. None can challenge anything from the Majesty on high without a warrant from Himself, nor could the conscience be satisfied unless it had a Divine grant for any good that we hope for from Him.

God will in all ages have His people regulated by His promises, so that they may exercise faith, hope, prayer, dependence upon Himself: He gives them promises so as to test them, whether or not they really trust in and count upon Him.

The Medium of the promises is the God-man Mediator, Jesus Christ, for there can be no intercourse between God and us except through the appointed Daysman. In other words, Christ must receive all good for us, and we must have it at second hand from Him.

Let the Christian ever be on his guard against contemplating any promise of God apart from Christ. Whether the thing promised, the blessing desired, be temporal or spiritual, we cannot legitimately or truly enjoy it except in and by Christ. Therefore did the Apostle remind the

Galatians, "Now to Abraham and his seed were the promises made. He saith not, And to seeds, as of many; but as of one, And to thy seed, which is Christ" (3:16)—in quoting

Genesis 12:3, Paul was not proving, but *affirming*, that God's promises to Abraham respected not all his natural posterity, but only those of his spiritual children—those united to Christ. All the promises of God to believers are made to Christ, the Surety of the everlasting covenant, and are conveyed from Him to us—both the promises themselves and the things promised. "This is *the* [all-inclusive] promise that He hath promised us, even eternal life" (1 John 2:25), and, as 5:11 tells us, "this life is in His Son"—so grace, and all other benefits. "If I read any of the promises I found that all and every one contained Christ in their bosom, He Himself being the one great Promise of the Bible. *To Him* they were all first given; *from Him* they derive all their efficacy, sweetness, value, and importance; *by Him* they are brought home to the heart; and *in Him* they are all yea, and amen" (R. Hawker, 1810).

Since all the promises of God are made in Christ, it clearly follows that none of them are available to any who are out of Christ, for to be out of Him is to be out of the favour of God. God cannot look on such a person but as an object of His wrath, as fuel for His vengeance: there is no hope for any man until he be in Christ. But it may be asked, Does not God bestow any good things on them who are out of Christ, sending His rain upon the unjust, and filling the bellies of the wicked with good things (Ps. 17:14)? Yes, He does indeed. Then are not those temporal mercies *blessings*? Certainly not: far from it. As He says in Malachi 2:2, "I will curse your blessings: yea, I have cursed them already, because ye do not lay it to heart" (cf. Deut. 28:15-20). Unto the wicked, the temporal mercies of God are like food given to bullocks—it does but "prepare them for the day of slaughter" (Jer. 12:3, and cf. Jam. 5:5).

Having presented above a brief outline on the subject of the Divine promises, let us now examine a striking yet little-noticed expression, namely "the children of the promise" (Rom. 9:8). In the context the Apostle discusses God's casting of the Jews and calling of the Gentiles, which was a particularly sore point with the former. After describing the unique privileges enjoyed by Israel as a nation (verses 4 and 5), he points out *the difference* there is between them and the antitypical "Israel of God" (verses 6-9), which he illustrates by the cases of Isaac and Jacob. Though the Jews had rejected the Gospel and had been cast off by God, it must not be supposed that His word had failed of accomplishment (verse 6), for not only had the prophecies concerning the Messiah been fulfilled, but the promise respecting Abraham's seed was being made good. But it was most important to apprehend aright what or *whom* that "seed" comprised. "For they are not all Israel [spiritually speaking], who are of Israel [naturally]: neither, because they are the seed of Abraham, are they all children: but, in Isaac shall thy seed be called" (verses 6 and 7).

The Jews erroneously imagined (as modern Dispensationalists do) that the promises made to Abraham concerning his seed respected all of his descendants. Their boast was "we be Abraham's seed" (John 8:33), to which Christ replied, "If ye were Abraham's children ye would do the works of Abraham" (verse 39 and see Romans 4:12). God's rejection of Ishmael and Esau was decisive proof that the promises were not made to the natural descendants as such. The selection of Isaac and Jacob showed that the promise was restricted to an elect line. "The children of the flesh, these are not the children of God; but the children of the promise are counted [regarded] as the seed. For this is the word of promise. At this time will I come, and Sarah shall have a son (Rom. 9:8,9). The "children of God" and the "children of promise" are one and the same, whether they be Jews or Gentiles. As Isaac was born supernaturally, so are all of God's elect (John 1:13). As Isaac, on that account, was heir of the promised blessing, so are Christians (Gal. 4:29; 3:29). "Children of the promise" are identical with "the heirs of promise" (Heb. 6:17, and cf. Rom. 8:17).

God's promises are made to the *spiritual children* of Abraham (Rom. 4:16; Gal 3:7), and none of them can possibly fail of accomplishment. "For *all* the promises of God in Him [namely Christ] are yea, and in Him amen" (2 Cor. 1:20). They are deposited in Christ, and in Him they find their affirmation and certification, for He is the sum and substance of them. Inexpressibly blessed is that declaration to the humble-minded child of God—yet a mystery hid from those who are wise in their own conceits.

"He that spared not His own Son, but delivered Him up for us all, how shall He not with Him also freely give us all things?" (Rom. 8:32). The promises of God are numerous: relating to this life and also that which is to come. They concern our temporal wellbeing, as well as our spiritual, covering the needs of the body as well as those of the soul. Whatever be their character, not one of them can be made good unto us except in and through and by Him who lived and died for us. The promises which God has given to His people are absolutely sure and trustworthy, for they were made to them in Christ: they are infallibly certain for fulfillment, for they are accomplished through and by Him.

A blessed illustration, yea, exemplification, of what has just been pointed out above is found in Hebrews 8:8-13, and 10:15-17, where the Apostle quotes the promises given in Jeremiah 31:31-34. The Dispensationalists would object and say that those promises belong to the natural descendants of Abraham, and are not to us. But Hebrews 10:15 prefaces the citation of those promises by expressly affirming, "Where of the Holy Spirit *is* [not "was"] a witness *to* us." Those promises extend to Gentile believers also, for they are the assurance of grace founded in Christ, and in Him believing Jews and Gentiles *are one* (Gal. 3:26). Before the middle wall of partition was broken down, Gentiles were indeed "strangers unto the covenants of promise" (Eph. 2:12), but when that wall was removed, Gentile believers became "fellow-heirs, and of the same body, and *partakers of* His promise in Christ by the gospel" (Eph. 3:6)! As Romans 11 expresses it, they partake of the root and fatness of the olive tree (verse 17)! Those promises in Jeremiah 31 are made not to the Jewish nation as such, but to "the Israel of God" (Gal 6:16), that is to the entire election of grace, and they are made infallibly good unto all of them at the moment of their regeneration by the Spirit.

In the clear light of other New Testament passages, it appears passing strange that anyone who is familiar with the same should deny that God has made this "new covenant" with those who are members of the mystical body of Christ. That Christians *are* partakers of its blessings is plain in 1 Corinthians 11:25, where quotation is made of the Savior's words at the institution of His supper, saying, "This cup is the new testament [or "new covenant"] in My blood"; and again by 2 Corinthians 3:6, where the Apostle states that God "hath also made us able ministers of the new testament," or "covenant," for the same Greek word is used in those passages as in Hebrews 8:8, and 10:16, where it is translated "covenant." In the very first sermon preached after the new covenant was established, Peter said, "For the promise is unto you, and to your children, and to all that are *afar off*" i.e. the Gentiles: Ephesians 2:13—qualified by "as many as the Lord our God shall call" (Acts 2:39). Furthermore, the terms of Jeremiah 31:33,34 are most certainly made good unto all believers *today*: God is their covenant God (Heb. 13:20), His law is enshrined in their affections (Rom 7:22), they know Him as their God, their iniquities are forgiven.

The Holy Spirit's statement in 2 Corinthians 7:1, must, for all who bow to the authority of Holy Writ, settle the matter once and for all of the Christian's right to the Old Testament promises. "Having therefore these promises, dearly beloved, let us cleanse ourselves from all filthiness of the flesh and spirit, perfecting holiness in the fear of God." *Which* promises? Why, those mentioned at the close of the preceding chapter. There we read, "And what agreement hath the temple of God with idols? for ye are the temple of the living God; *as God hath said*, I will dwell in them, and walk in them; and I will be their God, and they shall be My people" (6:16). And where had God said this? Why, as far back as Leviticus 26:12, "And I will walk among you, and will be your God, and ye shall be My people." That promise was made to the nation of Israel in the days of Moses! And again we read, "Wherefore come out from among them, and be ye separate, saith the Lord, and touch not the unclean thing; and I will receive you, and will be a Father unto you, and ye shall be My sons and daughters, saith the Lord Almighty" (2 Cor. 6:17, 18), which words are a manifest reference to Jeremiah 3 1:9, and Hosea 1:9,10.

Now observe very particularly what the Holy Spirit says through Paul concerning those Old Testament promises. First, he says to the New Testament saints, "Having these promises." He declared that those ancient promises are *theirs*: that they have a personal interest in them and title to them. That they were theirs not merely in hope, but in hand. Theirs to make full use of, to feed upon and enjoy, to delight in and give God thanks for the same. Since Christ Himself be ours, *all things* are ours (1 Cor. 3:22,23). Oh, Christian reader, suffer no man, under pretense of "rightly dividing the word," to cut you off from, to rob you of any of "the exceeding great and precious promises" of your Father (2 Pet. 1:4). If *he* is content to confine himself unto a few of the New Testament Epistles, let him do so—that is his loss. But allow him not to confine *you* to so narrow a compass. Second, we are hereby taught to use those promises as motives and incentives to the cultivation of personal piety, in the private work of mortification and the positive duty of practical sanctification.

A striking and conclusive proof that the Old Testament promises belong unto present-day saints is found in Hebrews 13:5, where practical use is again made of the same. There Christians are exhorted, "Let your conversation be without covetousness: be content with such things as ye have." That exhortation is enforced by this gracious consideration: "*for* He hath said, I will never leave thee, nor forsake thee." Since the living God be your portion your heart should rejoice in Him, and all anxiety about the supply of your every need be for ever removed. But what we are now more especially concerned with is the promise here cited: "For He hath said, I will never leave *thee*," etc. And to whom was that promise first given? Why, to the one who was about to lead Israel into the land of Canaan—as a reference to Joshua 1:5 shows. Thus it was made to a particular person on a special occasion, to a general who was to prosecute a great war under the immediate command of God. Facing that demanding ordeal, Joshua received assurance from God that His presence should ever be with him.

But if the believer gives way to unbelief, the devil is very apt to tell him, That promise belongs not unto you. *You* are not the captain of armies, commissioned by God to overthrow the forces of an enemy: the virtue of that promise ceased when Canaan was conquered and died with him to whom it was made. Instead, as Owen pointed out in his comments on Hebrews 13:5, "To manifest *the sameness* of love that is in all the promises, with their establishment in the one Mediator, and the general concern of believers in every one of them, howsoever and on what occasion given to any, this promise to Joshua is here applied to the condition of the weakest, meanest, and poorest of the saints; to all and every one of them, be their case and condition what it will. And doubtless, believers are not a little wanting in themselves and their own consolation, that they do so more particularly close with those words of truth, grace, and faithfulness, which upon sundry occasions and at divers times have been given out unto the saints of old, even Abraham, Isaac, Jacob, David, and the residue of them, who walked with God in their generation: these things in an especial manner are recorded for *our* consolation."

Let us now observe closely *the use* which the Apostle made of that ancient but ever-living promise. First, he here availed himself of it in order to enforce his exhortation unto Christians to the duties of mortification and sanctification. Second, he draws a logical and practical inference from the same, declaring, "*So that* we may boldly say, The Lord is my helper, and I will not fear what man shall do unto me" (Heb. 13:6). Thus a double conclusion is reached: such a promise is to inspire all believers with confidence in God's succour and assistance, and with boldness and courage before men—showing us to what purpose *we* should put the Divine pledges. Those conclusions are based upon the character of the Promiser: because God is infinitely good, faithful, and powerful, and because He changes not, I may trustfully declare with Abraham, "God will provide" (Gen. 22:8); with Jonathan, "There is no restraint to the Lord" (1 Sam. 14:6); with Jehoshaphat, "None is able to withstand Him" (2 Chron. 20:6); with Paul, "If God be for us, who can be against us?" (Rom 8:31). The abiding presence of the all-sufficient Lord ensures help, and therefore any alarm at man's enmity should be removed from our hearts. My worst enemy can do nothing against me without my Savior's permission.

"So that *we* may boldly say [freely, without hesitating through unbelief], The Lord is *my* helper, and I will not fear what man shall do unto me." Note attentively the change in number from the plural to the singular, and learn therefrom that general principles are to be appropriated by us in particular, as general precepts are to be taken by us personally—the Lord Jesus individualized the "*ye* shall not tempt the Lord your God" of Deuteronomy 6:16, when assailed by Satan, saying, "It is written again, *Thou* shalt not tempt the Lord thy God" (Matt. 4:7). It is only by taking the Divine promises and precepts unto ourselves personally that we can "mix faith" with the same, or make a proper and profitable use of them. It is also to be carefully noted that once more the Apostle confirmed his argument by a Divine testimony, for the words "The Lord is my helper, and I will not fear what man shall do unto me" are not his own, but a quotation of those use by David in Psalm 118:6. Thus again we are shown that the language of the Old Testament is exactly suited to the cases and circumstances of Christians today, and that it is their right and privilege freely to appropriate the same.

"We may boldly say" just what the Psalmist did when he was sorely pressed. It was during a season of acute distress that David expressed his confidence in the living God, at a time when it looked as though his enemies were on the point of swallowing him up; but viewing the omnipotence of Jehovah and contrasting His might with the feebleness of the creature, his heart was strengthened and emboldened. But let the reader clearly perceive what that implied. It means that David turned his mind away from the seen to the unseen. It means that he was regulated by faith, rather than by sight— feelings or reasonings. It means that his heart was occupied with the Almighty. But it means much more: he was occupied with *the relationship* of that omnipotent One unto himself. It means that he recognized and realized the spiritual bond there was between them, so that he could truly and rightly aver, "the Lord is my helper." If He be my God, my Redeemer, my Father, then He may be counted upon to undertake for me when I am sorely oppressed, when my foes threaten to devour me, when my barrel of meal is almost empty. That "my" is the language of faith, and is the conclusion which faith's assurance draws from the infallible promise of Him that cannot lie.

Chapter 5

In these articles we are seeking to show the *use* which believers should make of God's Word: or more particularly, how that it is both their privilege and their duty to receive *the whole of it* as addressed immediately *unto themselves*, and to turn the same unto practical account, by appropriating its contents to their personal needs. The Bible is a book which calls not so much for the exertion of our intellect as it does for the exercise of our affections, conscience and will. God has given it to us not for our entertainment but for our education, to make known what He requires from us. It is to be the traveler's guide as he journeys through the maze of this world, the mariner's chart as he sails the sea of life. Therefore, whenever we open the Bible, the all-important consideration for each of us to keep before him is, What is there here *for me* today? What bearing does the passage now before me have upon my present case and circumstances—what warning, what encouragement, what information? What instruction is there to direct me in the management of my business, to guide me in the ordering of my domestic and social affairs, to promote a closer walking with God?

I should see myself addressed in every precept, included in every promise. But it is greatly to be feared that, through failure to appropriate God's Word unto their own case and circumstances, there is much Bible reading and study which is of little or no real benefit to the soul. Nothing else will secure us from the infections of this world, deliver from the temptations of Satan, and be so effectual a preservative from sin, as the Word of God received into our affections. "The law of his God is *in his heart*; none of his steps shall slide" (Ps. 37:31) can only be said of the one who has made personal appropriation of that Law, and is able to aver with the Psalmist,

37

"Thy word have I hid in mine heart, that I might not sin against Thee" (119:11). Just so long as the Truth is actually working in us, influencing us in a practical way, is loved and revered by us, stirs the conscience, are we kept from falling into open sin—as Joseph was preserved when evilly solicited by his master's wife (Gen. 39:9). And only as we personally go out and daily gather our portion of manna, and feed upon the same, will there be strength provided for the performing of duty and the bringing forth of fruit to the glory of God.

Let us take Genesis 17:1 as a simple illustration. "And when Abram was ninety years old and nine, the Lord appeared to Abram and said unto him, I am the Almighty God; walk before Me, and be thou perfect" or "sincere." *How* is the Christian to apply such a verse *unto himself?* First of all, let him note to whom this signal favour and honour was shown: namely to him who is the "father of all them that believe" (Rom. 4:11,12,16)—and he was the first person in the world to whom the Lord is said to have appeared! Second, observe when it was that Jehovah appeared unto him: namely in his old age, when nature's force was spent and death was written on the flesh. Third, mark attentively the particular character in which the Lord was now revealed to him: "the Almighty God," or more literally *"El Shaddai"*—"the all-sufficient God." Fourth, consider the exhortation which accompanied the same: "walk before Me, and be thou sincere." Fifth, ponder those details in the light of the immediate sequel; God's making promise that he should beget a son by Sarah, who was long past the age of child-bearing (verses 15-19). Everything that is *for* God must be effected by His mighty power: He can and must do everything—the flesh profits nothing, no movement of mere nature is of any avail.

Now as the believer ponders that memorable incident, *hope* should be inspired within him. *El Shaddai* is as truly *his* God as He was Abraham's! That is clear from 2 Corinthians 7:1, for one of those promises is, "I will be a Father unto you.... .saith the Lord Almighty" (6:18), and from Revelation 1:8, where the Lord Jesus says unto the churches, "I am Alpha and Omega... .the Almighty." It is a declaration of His omnipotence, to whom all things are possible. "The all-sufficient God" tells of what He is in Himself—independent, self-existent; and what He is unto His people—the Supplier of their every need. When Christ said to Paul, "My grace *is sufficient* for thee," it was all one with what Jehovah said unto Abraham. Doubtless the Lord appeared unto the patriarch in visible (and human) form: He does so to us before the eyes of faith. Often He is pleased to meet with us in the ordinances of His grace, and send us on our way rejoicing. Sometimes He "manifests" Himself (John 14:21) to us in the retirements of privacy. Frequently He appears *for us* in His providences, showing Himself strong on our behalf. Now, says He, "Walk before Me sincerely" in the believing realization that I am all-sufficient for thee, conscious of My almightiness, and all will be well with thee.

Let us now adduce some of the many *proofs* of the assertions made in our opening sentences, proofs supplied by the Holy Spirit and the Lord Jesus in the application which They made of the Scriptures. It is very striking indeed to discover that the very first moral commandment which God gave to mankind, namely that which was to regulate the marriage relationship, was couched in such terms that it comprehended a Divine law which is universally and perpetually binding: "Therefore shall a man leave his father and mother, and shall cleave unto his wife; and they shall be one flesh" (Gen. 2:24)—quoted by Christ in Matthew 19:5. "When a man hath taken a wife, and married her, and it come to pass that she find no favor in his eyes, because he hath found some uncleanness in her: then let him write her a bill of divorcement" (Deut. 24:1). That statute was given in the days of Moses, nevertheless we find our Lord referring to the same and telling the Pharisees of His day, "For the hardness of your heart he wrote *you* this precept" (Mark 10:5).

The principle for which we are here contending is beautifully illustrated in Psalm 27:8, "When Thou saidst, Seek ye My face; my heart said unto Thee, Thy face, Lord, will I seek." Thus David made particular what was general, applying to himself personally what was said to the saints collectively. That is ever the use each of us should make of every part of God's Word—as we see the Saviour in Matthew 4:7, changing the "ye" of Deuteronomy 6:16, to "thou." So again in Acts 1:20, we find Peter, when alluding to the defection of Judas, altering the "let *their* habitation" of Psalm 69:25, to "let *his* habitation be desolate." That was not taking an undue liberty with Holy Writ, but, instead, making a specific application of what was indefinite.

"Put not forth thyself in the presence of the king, and stand not in the place of great men: for better it is that it be said unto thee, Come up hither; than that thou shouldest be put lower in the presence of the prince whom thine eyes have seen" (Prov. 25:6,7). Upon which Thomas Scott justly remarked, "There can be no reasonable doubt that our Lord referred to those words in His admonition to ambitious guests at the Pharisee's table (Luke 14:7-11), and was understood to do so. While, therefore, this gives His sanction to the book of Proverbs, it also shows that those maxims may be applied to similar cases, and that we need not confine their interpretation exclusively to the subject which gave rise to the maxims." Not even the presence of Christ, His holy example, His heavenly instruction, could restrain the strife among His disciples over which should be the greatest. Loving to have the pre-eminence (3 John 9,10) is the bane of godliness in the churches.

"I the Lord have called Thee... . and give Thee for a covenant of the people, for a light of the Gentiles"; "I will also give Thee for a light to the Gentiles, that Thou mayest be My salvation unto the end of the earth" (Isa. 42:6; 49:6). Those words were spoken by the Father unto the Messiah, yet in Acts 13:46,47 we find Paul saying of himself and Barnabas, "Lo, we turn to the Gentiles. For so bath the Lord commanded *us*; saying, I have set thee to be a light of the Gentiles, that thou shouldest be for salvation unto the ends of the earth"! So again in Romans 10:15 we find the Apostle was inspired to make application unto Christ's servant of that which was said immediately of Him: "How beautiful upon the mountains are the feet of *Him* that bringeth good tidings, that publisheth peace" (Isa. 52:7): "How shall they preach, except they be sent? as it is written, How beautiful are the feet of *them* that preach the gospel of peace" (Rom. 10:15). "He is near that justifieth Me... . who is he that shall condemn Me?" (Isa. 50:8,9): the context shows unmistakably that Christ is there the speaker, yet in Romans 8:33, 34 the Apostle hesitates not to apply those words unto the members of His body: "Who shall lay any thing to the charge of God's elect? It is God that justifieth. Who is he that condemneth?"

The unspeakably solemn commission given to Isaiah concerning his apostate generation (6:9,10) was applied by Christ to the people of His day, saying: "And *in them* is fulfilled the prophecy of Isaiah" (Matt. 13:14,15).

Again, in 29:13, Isaiah announced that the Lord said, "This people draw near Me with their mouth, and with their lips do honour Me, but have removed their heart far from Me," while in Matthew 15:7 we find Christ saying to the scribes and Pharisees, "Hypocrites, well did Isaiah prophesy *of you*, saying, This people draweth nigh unto Me with their mouth," etc. Even more striking is Christ's rebuke unto the Sadducees, who denied the resurrection of the body, "Have ye not read that which was *spoken unto you* by God, saying, I am the God of Abraham, and the God of Isaac, and the God of Jacob? God is not the God of the dead, but of the living" (Matt. 22:31,32). What God spoke immediately to Moses at the burning bush was designed equally for the instruction and comfort of all men unto the end of the world. What the Lord has said unto a particular person, He says unto everyone who is favored to read His Word. Thus does it concern us to hear and heed the same, for by that Word we shall be judged in the last great day (John 12:48).

The fundamental principle for which we are here contending is plainly expressed again by Christ in Mark 13:37, "And what I say unto you I say unto all, Watch." That exhortation to the Apostles is addressed directly to the saints in all generations and places. As Owen well said, "The Scriptures speak to every age, every church, every person, not less than to those to whom they were first directed. This showeth us how we should be affected in reading the Word: we should read it as a letter written by the Lord of grace from heaven, *to us by name*." If there be any books in the New Testament particularly restricted, it is the "pastoral Epistles," yet the exhortation found in 2 Timothy 2:19, is generalized: "*Let everyone* that nameth the name of Christ depart from iniquity." Those who are so fond of restricting God's Word would say that, "Thou therefore endure hardness, as a good soldier of Jesus Christ" (verse 3) is addressed to the minister of the Gospel, and pertains not to the rank and file of believers. But Ephesians 6:10-17 shows (by necessary implication) that it applies to *all* the saints, for the militant figure is again used, and used there without limitation. The Bullinger school insist that James and Peter—who gave warning of those who in the last time should walk after their own ungodly lusts—wrote to Jewish believers; but Jude (addressed to all the sanctified) declares they "told *you*" (verse 18).

"Ye have forgotten the exhortation which speaketh unto you as unto children, My son, despise not thou the chastening of the Lord" (Heb. 12:5). That exhortation is taken from Proverbs 3:11, so that here is further evidence that the precepts of the Old Testament (like its promises) are not restricted unto those who were under the Mosaic economy, but apply with equal directness and force to those under the new covenant. Observe well the tense of the verb "which *speaketh*": though written a thousand years previously, Paul did not say "which hath spoken"—the Scriptures are a living Word through which their Author speaks *today*. Note too "which speaketh *unto you*"—New Testament saints: all that is contained in the book of Proverbs is as truly and as much the Father's instruction to Christians as the contents of the Pauline Epistles. Throughout that book God addresses us individually as "My son" (2:1; 3:1; 4:1; 5:1). That exhortation is as urgently needed by believers now as by any who lived in former ages. Though children of God, we are still children of Adam—willful, proud, independent, requiring to be disciplined, to be under the Father's rod, to bear it meekly, and to be exercised thereby in our hearts and consciences.

A word now upon *transferred application*, by which we mean giving a literal turn to language which is figurative, or vice versa. Thus, whenever the writer steps on to icy roads, he hesitates not to literalize the prayer, "Hold Thou me up, and I shall be safe" (Ps. 119:117). "I will both lay me down in peace, and sleep: for Thou, Lord, only makest me dwell in safety" (Ps. 4:8) is to be given its widest latitude, and regarded at both the rest of the body under the protection of Providence and the repose of the soul in the assurance of God's protecting grace. In 2 Corinthians 8:14 Paul urges that there should be an equality of giving, or a fair distribution of the burden, in the collection being made to relieve the afflicted saints in Jerusalem. That appeal was backed up with, "As it is written, he that hath gathered much had nothing over; and he that had gathered little had no lack." That is a reference to the manna gathered by the Israelites (Ex. 16:18): those who gathered the largest quantity had more to give unto the aged and feeble; so rich Christians should use their surplus to provide for the poor of the flock. But great care needs to be taken lest we clash with the Analogy of the Faith: thus "the house of Saul waxed weaker and weaker" (2 Sam. 3:1) certainly does not mean that "the flesh" becomes enervated as the believer grows in grace, for universal Christian experience testifies that indwelling sin rages as vigorously at the end as at the beginning.

A brief word upon *double application*. Whereas preachers should ever be on their guard against taking the children's bread and casting it to the dogs, by applying to the unsaved promises given to or statements made concerning the saints; on the other hand, they need to remind believers of the *continuous force* of the Scriptures and their present suitability to their cases. For instance, the gracious invitation of Christ, "Come unto Me, all ye that labour and are heavy laden, and I will give you rest" (Matt. 11:28), and "If any man thirst, let him come unto Me, and drink" (John 7:37), must not be limited to our first approach to the Saviour as lost sinners, but as 1 Peter 2:4 says, "to whom coming"—in the present tense. Note too the "mourn" and not "have mourned" in Matthew 5:4, and "hunger" in verse 6. In like manner, the self-abasing word, "Who maketh thee to differ!" (1 Cor. 4:7) today: first from the unsaved; second from what *we* were before the new birth; and third from other Christians with less grace and gifts. Why, a sovereign God, and therefore you have nothing to boast of and no cause for self-glorying.

A word now upon *the Spirit's application* of the Word unto the heart, and our task is completed. This is described in such a verse as, "For our gospel came not unto you in word only, but also in power, and in the Holy Spirit, and in much assurance" (1 Thess. 1:5). That is very much more than having the mind informed or the emotions stirred, and something radically different from being deeply impressed by the preacher's oratory, earnestness, etc. It is for the preaching of the Gospel to be accompanied by the supernatural operation of the Spirit, and the efficacious grace of God, so that souls are Divinely quickened, convicted, converted, delivered from the dominion of sin and Satan. When the Word is applied by the Spirit to a person, it acts like the entrance of a two-edged sword into his inner man, piercing, wounding, slaying his self-complacency and self-righteousness— as in the case of Saul of Tarsus (Rom. 7:9,10). This is the "demonstration of the Spirit" (1 Cor. 2:4), whereby He gives proof of the Truth by the effects produced in the individual to which it is sayingly applied, so that he has "much assurance"—i.e. he *knows* it is *God's Word* because of the radical and permanent change wrought in him.

Now the child of God is in daily need of this gracious working of the Holy Spirit: to make the Word work "effectually" (1 Thess. 2:13) within his soul and truly regulate his life, so that he can thankfully acknowledge, "I will never forget Thy precepts: for with them Thou hast *quickened me*" (Ps. 119:93). For that quickening it is his duty and privilege to pray (verses 25, 37, 40, 88, 107, 149, etc.). It is a fervent request that he may be "renewed day by day" in the inner man (2 Cor. 4:16), that he may be "strengthened with might by His Spirit" (Eph. 3:16), that he may be revived and animated to go in the path of God's commandments (Ps. 119:35). It is an earnest petition that his heart may be awed by a continual sense of God's majesty, and melted by a realization of His goodness, so that he may see light in God's light, recognizing the evil in things forbidden and the blessedness of the things enjoined. "Quicken Thou me" is a prayer for vitalizing grace, that he may be taught to profit (Isa. 48:17), for the increasing of his faith, the strengthening of his expectations, the firing of his zeal. It is equivalent to "draw me, we will run after Thee" (Song 1:4).

Made in the USA
San Bernardino, CA
06 January 2018